# Nature's Touch

## Basketry by Hand
## from Pine Needles and Gourds

## Vicky Nickelson

MOONLIGHT GARDEN PUBLICATIONS

Renton, Washington

Published 2014, Moonlight Garden Publications.

Photography by Vicky Nickelson.
Edited by S. C. Moore and C. E. Moore.

ISBN: 978-1-938281-70-9  (paperback)
ISBN: 978-1-938281-71-6  (e-book)

Library of Congress Control Number:  2014947394

Moonlight Garden Publications is an imprint of
Gazebo Gardens Publishing, LLC.
www.GazeboGardensPublishing.com

Printed in the United States of America.

# ACKNOWLEDGEMENTS

I would like to thank my patient and encouraging husband, Ron. His help has made this book possible. A special appreciation for my parents for that camping trip where I learned to make pine needle baskets and for all of their "Gathering." For my Sons, Joe and Tim, who could not wait to get to the fair to see the ribbons Mom's baskets won. My brother, Mike, for the many road trips to gather supplies. My sister, Kim, who is always showing off my baskets. I am very grateful to John Simunds for his encouragement to write this book and his interest and amazement that pine needles can be made into baskets. I am very grateful to my author friend, Dianna Stevens, for all her tips and help. A special thank you to my friend, Valerie Holton, who has been my agent, motivator, and promoter. To Fritzi for letting me borrow the figure eight tray from her private collection, to feature in this book. And to Sue Marvin, who has inspired many basketmakers, including myself.

# TABLE OF CONTENTS

# INTRODUCTION

There are many books available on beading, stitching, quilting, tole painting, etc.; only a handful of books are available on pine needle baskets and even fewer on gourd baskets or vessels. You may find a few limited articles in your "something for everyone" craft book. I hope to introduce you to one of nature's crafts, *Basketry by Hand from Pine Needles and Gourds.*

You can find much enjoyment in gathering pine needles and searching your local garden markets for gourds. Gathering can be hard work, but completing your basket is very rewarding. Remember to photograph your masterpiece. The type of photo you take will depend on what you plan on doing with your basket. Publishers generally like high contrast black and white photographs, while juried art shows request slides. Don't forget the color pictures for your scrapbook and friends!

Thanks to nature, each basket you create with gourds is unique, as no two gourds are ever the same. The instructions you receive in this book will be as accurate as possible with the dimensions of the gourd given. You will need to make adjustments to accommodate your gourd. Let your own creativity take over! Pine needle baskets will also have their own uniqueness due to color and size variation of pine needles. The wire shape, raffia, and gauge used also play an important part in sizing.

Basketry predates pottery and weaving in our history. Baskets date back to 9000 BC. They have been unearthed from ancient granaries in Egypt, and the arid climate probably helped preserve them. I am happy to say basketry is not a dying art. The variations are endless, from rustic to elegant, functional to nonfunctional. With a little patience and a lot of imagination, we are ready to begin. If you are a beginner or a basketmaker looking to try new materials, I hope you enjoy transforming pine needles and gourds into works of art. I have included a variety of projects for your enjoyment..

# Section One

## Pine Needle Basketry

# PINE NEEDLES

There are more than ninety recognized species of the pine tree. Most of these are native to the Northern Hemisphere, and about thirty species are native to the United States. Each pine tree has two kinds of leaves, also known as needles: the primary and the secondary. Secondary needles grow in bundles from the area between the leaf and stem of the primary needles, which form a papery sheath at the base of each pine needle bundle. The sheath end is generally removed before stitching.

Needles can be anywhere from one to eighteen inches long, and any pine needles over six inches may be used for basketmaking. Needles less than six inches are difficult to work with and do not hold their shape well in a basket. There are multiple species of pine trees with long needles suitable for baskets. Many are probably right in your back yard. The Ponderosa and the Longleaf Pine are my favorites.

The Ponderosa, or Western Yellow Pine (*Pinus ponderosa*), is one of the most important pine trees in basket coiling. Its needles are four to ten inches long. It is widely distributed from British Columbia to Mexico, growing in every state west of the Great Plains. It is also the state tree of Montana.

The Longleaf Pine (*Pinus palustris*), is an important southern timber tree and a source of turpentine. Its needles are eight to eighteen inches long; therefore, they are the most desired and sought after for baskets. The tree is found on coastal plains from Virginia to Florida and west to Texas, and its needles are often available for purchase.

## Gathering and Preparing Pine Needles

Gathering pine needles is how we collect our supply for future use. It is best to gather in the late summer or early fall before the rainy season is upon us. It is not necessary to climb trees or reach for branches. Just gather them from the ground! Mother Nature has already dried them and turned them a beautiful golden brown color for us. A yard or park that has been groomed is generally the best, as the needles are freshly fallen.

Try not to gather needles that have been exposed to the weather for extended periods; these tend to have mold or decay spots. Green needles should not be used. The shrinkage during the drying stage will cause your stitches to become loose, no matter how tight you stitch them. You may dry green needles on a screen in the shade if desired. This process usually takes about two weeks.

To gather, collect a handful of needles, sheath ends facing the same direction, and rubber band each end to keep the needles from twisting. You may also tie each end with string or fill an empty toilet paper roll. Store the needles in a cool, dry place. Your needles will keep indefinitely if stored properly. Make sure you find enough to last until the next gathering season. A medium-sized basket normally requires about 8 oz. or a six-inch bundle of pine needles. Don't take the fun out of your hobby by counting needles! After you have stitched a few baskets, you'll have a better idea of how many pine needles are required.

I would like to share with you one of life's lessons in gathering. My parents are retired and travel in their motor home. They always leave home with instructions from me to be on the lookout for Longleaf pine needles. One afternoon, they pulled into a beautiful campground in North Carolina. After settling in, they decided to take a walk and check out the campground. They discovered the lawn was full of freshly fallen Longleaf pine needles. Excited to find some needles, they started gathering. Unfortunately, dusk was falling, and the mosquitoes were beginning to feed. They decided to call it a night and continue in the morning but woke up to the sound of the lawn mower! The moral of this story is: when you find an excellent gathering place, no matter what, gather!

To begin your basket, the needles need to be flexible. Soak your needles in cold water for approximately one hour prior to starting your basket. If using hot water, shorten the time to twenty or thirty minutes. Don't leave the needles soaking for long periods of time; they absorb too much water, and then we're back to the shrinkage problem. Use the dampened needles on the base coil for about two inches. Switch to dry needles to prevent the basket from being unstable due to shrinkage. You may keep the extra-dampened needles in an airtight container for about one week in the refrigerator. Be sure to mark the date, as an extended stay will cause decay. While the needles are soaking, use this time to gather the rest of your supplies and critique your design.

The next few pages will introduce you to the basket beginnings and stitches used. You will learn to create a basket either from the patterns included in this book or your own design.

Each basket is a simple technique of coiling continuous coils of pine needles to themselves. I suggest you try all the basket beginnings to find your favorite. Beginning a basket can be the most difficult part. Don't let that discourage you from trying the stitches.

A variety of threads are available for stitching pine needle baskets. The most common and frequently used is raffia, a natural material that compliments the pine needles. Raffia tends to fray and requires some prep work. To prepare it, straighten the fibers with your hands and split it a quarter-inch wide by piercing it with a sharp sewing needle. Thread the needle with the stem end (thick end) to help prevent it from shredding when it is drawn through the pine needles. Waxed linen may also be used. It is very strong and can be purchased in an array of colors. No prep work is required for the waxed linen. Artificial sinew is another choice and is similar to raffia. It can be split very thin and is excellent when adding beads to a teneriffe pattern or the fagoting stitch. It also has many color options to choose from. Artificial sinew may be used to stitch a basket or split thin for miniature baskets and fine detailed work.

## Materials and Supplies

Pine needle basketmaking is a very affordable hobby. The end results are priceless! I have listed some general supplies to help you get started. You may not need all of them for a basket. Experiment with different styles of beginnings and stitches to create a style all your own. I prefer the look of raffia you may substitute your choice of thread in any of the patterns.

Size 6 tapestry needle
Size 16 embroidery needle
Artificial sinew
Wire shapes (galvanized wire)
Container in which to soak pine needles
3/16-inch copper compression sleeve gauge
    (optional)

Pine needles
Raffia (see note)
Waxed linen
Walnut slices
Scissors
Tape measure

*Note: Raffia comes from the leaves of the Raffia Palm in Madagascar, Africa. You can purchase either East Coast or West Coast raffia. The East Coast raffia generally comes in pigtail form and is slightly shorter. The West Coast raffia, which is my preference, is the best there is and referred to as extra fancy. It is available by the hank.*

Once you have the pine needles gathered and the supplies at hand, you are ready to begin. You will start with the double buttonhole wrapped ring or a pine needle wrapped beginning.

## Buttonhole Stitch

This stitch provides the necessary two rows of loops for making teneriffe patterns and to begin the pine needle basket base from. You may choose galvanized wire shapes or plastic rings to begin your wrap on.

Begin by selecting a long fiber of raffia 1/4 inch wide (or waxed linen). Fold the raffia in half. Lay the fold under the ring. The fold should be in the center of the ring. Pull both ends through the loop formed.

You will have formed a lark's head knot.

Place the knot on the right side of the ring. Separate the ends. Place the left strand across the ring to the left and the right strand to the right of the ring. Take the right strand across the front of the ring, forming a loop. Push the end down through the ring, around and up through the loop. Slide the strand up to rest below the lark's head knot.

To complete the first step of the buttonhole stitch, bring your left strand up through the center of the ring. Be sure the strand is below the strand itself. Slide this stitch around to rest below the right hand stitch and pull it snug. Begin each stitch starting with the right strand and completing with the left.

Repeat around the ring.

Add new thread when the tail is 3 inches long. Choose another piece of raffia or desired thread. Find the middle of the new thread and lay it behind your last stitch. Work with the old and new thread for about three stitches. Leave the old thread behind and continue around with the new. Cut off the old thread close to the ring.

Work your stitches up to meet the first buttonhole stitch made. Thread the right strand into a sewing needle. Sew into the first loop of the first buttonhole stitch. Weave in and out of several loops to secure. Thread the left strand and repeat the steps. Cut off the ends of both threads close to the form.

# Teneriffe Weaving

**Spokes:** Spokes are placed in the opening of a form in order to weave a design. A teneriffe pattern is created on spokes to fill in the open spaces and to add a touch of beauty and elegance to a basket. The number of spokes needed for the pattern determines the spacing of the spokes. To create a spoke, first select a piece of raffia 1/8 inch wide and thread a sewing needle. Utilizing the outside edge loops of the buttonhole stitch, weave in and out a few loops to secure the thread. Come across the backside of the ring and bring the needle and thread through the inside loop.

**Fifteen-Spoke Form:** Begin by dividing the ring in half. Take a stitch directly across the ring from front to back. Weave in out about three loops on the outside of the ring, about 1/8 inch. Come across the back side and bring the needle and thread from the back to the front.

Bisect the ring again and cross over the first spoke. Pass the needle and thread from front to back (Diagram 2), 1/8 inch to the right of the first spoke. Weave in and out the outside loops again. Cross over the back and bring the needle and thread from back to front, 1/8 inch from the previous spoke (Diagram 3). Continue bisecting the ring until you have fifteen spokes. To make the fifteenth and last spoke, come across to the center only and tie an overhand knot in the middle on the back side, going around all the spokes (Diagram 4).

Diagram 2

Diagram 3

Diagram 4

**Three-Leaf or Arrow Pattern:** Begin with fifteen spokes. Work from the center out. Start with five spokes; weave from the right to the left. Go under the first, over the second, under the third, over the fourth, and under the fifth. Turn and weave back across in the same manner. Weave the five spokes one quarter of the way down.

Drop the first and fifth spokes and weave on the center three spokes. Work down until a small space remains.

Bring the needle and thread up through the weaving along the spoke to the center position.

From the center position, continue weaving the next two leaves or arrows. Work each leaf on five spokes. This diagram shows the completed three-leaf or arrow pattern.

*Note: These examples are done with waxed linen and sinew for the contrast. I prefer the look of raffia wrapped around the ring and for the teneriffe patterns. Be creative and find what works and looks the best for you!*

**Three-Leaf Swirl Pattern:** Start with fifteen spokes and work from the center out. Begin with five spokes; weave from right to left. Go under the first, over the second, under the third, over the fourth, and under the fifth. Turn and weave back from left to right. Go over the first, under the second, over the third, under the fourth, and over the fifth. Repeat the process.

Work the five spokes down one quarter of the way.

Drop the fifth spoke (far left spoke) in the weaving. Continue weaving a quarter of the way down. Now drop the fourth spoke and weave another quarter way down. Drop the third spoke and weave on the last two spokes. Work down until a small space remains. This diagram shows one completed swirl leaf.

Dropping a spoke each step down, bring the needle and thread up through the weaving along the spoke to the center position.

From the center position, continue weaving the next two leaves to fill in the ring. Always drop a spoke on the left side. This creates the swirling effect of the pattern.

**Figure Eight Pattern:** The figure eight is a stunning way to begin a basket. It can be used alone, or additional wrapped buttonhole rings may be attached. To attach the rings together, utilize the outside buttonhole loops. With the desired thread, stitch in and out of the buttonhole loops to link them together. A bread tie will help hold the forms together during stitching.

To begin, buttonhole stitch a figure eight form. Once this is completed, start the pattern, which is made with five spokes on each side. Attach the raffia, using the outside loop to secure. Bring the raffia across the back and come up in the center inside loop. Go directly across the midline and attach the raffia where the form crosses. This makes the first spoke. Come back across the form and attach the second spoke about 1/4 inch from the first. Weave in and out of the loops to get in position for the third spoke. Repeat for a total of five spokes, each going through the same hole at the cross.

Begin weaving where all five spokes meet. Go under the first, over the second, under the third, over the fourth, and under the fifth. Turn and weave back across. Weave down about half way. Drop the first and fifth spoke and weave on the center three spokes until a small space remains.

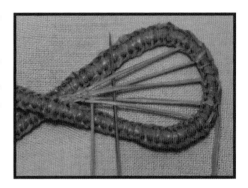

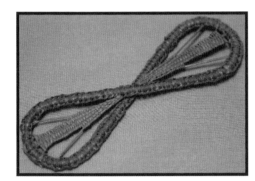

Repeat the design in the other half. See the figure eight tray on page 21 for an example on how to use this form.

## Wrapped Beginnings

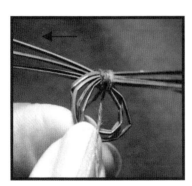

Start with pre-soaked pine needles. Use four to five individual needles, with all the pointed ends together. Form a loop on the blunt end and hold it with your left thumb. If the pine needles break, you need to soak them longer. Have the blunt ends to your right and the pointed ends to your left. Bring the thread up through the center of the pine needle ring, leaving a tail. Wrap the thread around from front to back to bind the ring together. After a few wraps once the ring is secure, make the circle smaller by pulling on both ends of the pine needles. If the needles are not pulled evenly, you can adjust each one individually.

Cut the blunt ends (right side) of the pine needles.

Continue wrapping, covering the cut ends until the circle is completely covered.

To secure your thread, take a stitch in the edge of the ring. Now, select your desired stitch. This is the place that will mark where you make changes. From this mark you shape, change stitches and end the basket. The chain stitch is shown here. It makes a swirling effect when done on a circular base. See the pattern for the Pine Needle Pendant, beginning on page 24.

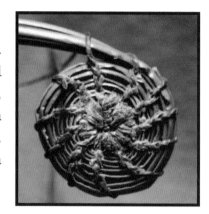

*Note:* In the first row, the stitches are placed very closely together. As the circle grows, the stitches will be further apart. Place the first row of stitches evenly so an evenly-spaced spiral will form.

## Basic Pine Needle Stitches

The stitches illustrated are some of the basic stitches included in the patterns within this book. Please realize these are not the only stitches available in pine needle basketry. Many others have been created for the interested basketmaker. You may even choose to create your own stitch.

**Chain or Whip Stitch:** This is used primarily on small, flat pieces. It is also a great stitch to use when adding a rim of pine needles around a gourd. It is a one-part stitch. Bring the needle and thread from the back to the front and pierce through the stitch below. Overcast around the row and pierce through the next stitch. Split the stitch in the previous row about half way down into the row.

**Wheat Stitch:** This is my favorite and the most basic stitch. It is a two-part stitch. Overcast from front to back, then pierce the thread in the previous row about half way down. This creates the straight up and down part of the stitch. To make the slant portion, overcast again. Pierce the straight part of the stitch in the previous row about half way down. To give the stitch on open V look, bring the needle and thread up between the two parts of the stitch on the previous row (instead of piercing through the straight part of the stitch). Be sure the needle pierces half way through the previous row to keep the stitch secure.

**Swirling Wheat Stitch:** A beautiful stitch for a tray bottom or lid top, though the reverse side is not very becoming. Create the swirling pattern by using the wheat stitch, but pierce through the slant portion of the stitch instead of the straight portion. To emphasize the swirling effect, use wide spacing.

**Fern Stitch:** This is a very strong stitch and helps hold in all the pine needle ends. For this reason, it should be used on the rim to finish your basket. It may also be used to add extra stability in a basket. It is a three-part stitch. First, complete one row of the wheat stitch. When you reach the end of the row, do a chain stitch back to the right. Come up at the base of each wheat stitch or at the point of the V.

**Fagoting Stitch:** This stitch is used to add strength and to fill in open spaces. It also adds a touch of elegance to a basket. If using raffia, use the thinner rope sides of the raffia. Attach the thread to one end of the opening. Take a stitch from the front to the back (if stitching on a basket). The illustration is done on a wire form to make it easier for you to see. Take the needle and thread at an angle across the open space. Bring the needle and thread

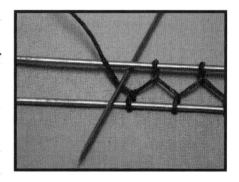

from the back to the front, passing to the right of the thread. (If working right to left, reverse it for left to right.) Take the needle and thread back across the space at an angle and take a stitch from front to back. Bring the needle and thread to the right side of the thread again and repeat across the open space.

**Adding Beads:** As an extra touch, try adding seed beads to the fagoting stitch. (For the benefit of this example, I've used a larger bead.) If using raffia, choose a very thin but durable rope side of the raffia, or try sinew. Use a size 13 beading needle and size 11 seed beads of your choice. Before taking the first stitch, add a seed bead to the thread. Take your stitch from front to back.

Pass the needle and thread to the right of the stitch (if working right to left) and go back down through the seed bead. Add another seed bead and take the next stitch. Repeat until the space is filled.

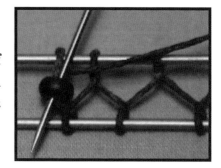

# Attaching the Pine Needle Coil
## to a Wrapped Form

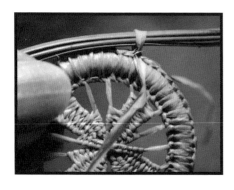

Begin with a wrapped form with the teneriffe weave completed. Have the right side of the form facing you. Start with pre-soaked pine needles for flexibility. Cut off the nub end of two clusters of pine needles. Place all the pointed ends facing the same direction. Stagger the points for less bulk. Attach your thread by going in and out a few buttonhole loops. Lay the pine needle coil on top of the form and thread with the blunt ends to your left. With your thread overcast around the coil from front to back, come out in the same buttonhole stitch. Overcast again to make sure the coil is secure. The pointed ends should extend about ½ inch past the overcast stitch to the right.

Monitor your coil and add new pine needles as needed. Don't let them run out at the same time. To add a new pine needle, insert the pointed end, ribbed side down, into the middle of the coil. The wheat stitch is shown in this diagram.

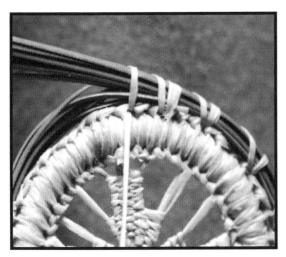

As you come around, tuck the loose ends of the pine needles under the coil. When you come back around to the first stitch, make the next stitch by inserting the needle and thread into the middle of the previous stitch. This is the mark you use to keep the basket symmetrical. From this mark, change stitches and end the basket. With your choice of stitch, continue around to coil a flat disc by placing each coil on the outside edge of the previous row. Use pre-soaked needles only far enough to prevent breaking.

## Ending and Adding New Thread

There comes a time when that piece of thread is at its end. When ENDING, simply bring the needle and thread up through the coil and come out on top of the coil in the middle of the straight stitch. Leave a tail and hide it in the next coil as you go around.

When ADDING a new thread, first knot the end of the thread. Next, bring the needle and thread back down through the last stitch and come out in the bottom of the stitch. For added strength, I overcast around the straight portion of the stitch and come out at the same point where I left off.

Once the add is COMPLETED, the tail and knot will be hidden by your next coiled row.

# Shaping and Ending Your Basket

SHAPING is all in the placement of the coil. There are four main shapes I will detail for you here.

To create a FLAT DISC coil from the center out, place each coil on the outside edge of the previous row. Do not roll it to the front or back, or you will have a bowl.

To begin STRAIGHT UP THE SIDES, lay your pine needle coil up on top of the previous coil. Continue laying each new coil on top of the previous coil.

For FLARED OR ANGLED SIDES, lay your coil on top of the flat disc at an angle. Continue laying each coil at an angle away from you.

To FLARE IN OR PULL IN THE SIDES, lay the coil at an angle to the inside of the basket on the previous row.

When ENDING your basket, look for the beginning indicator on the last row. At 3 inches from the indicator, stop adding pine needles and taper to an end. Overcast around the last stitch a couple of times. If using the wheat stitch, move to the right with the chain stitch to create the fern stitch. This will give added strength to the rim of your basket.

Shellacking a basket is the final step. Shellac is applied to preserve and protect your basket. You may also choose to leave your basket as is. Care should be taken not to handle the basket and keep it out of direct sunlight. Mix equal parts of half denatured alcohol solvent and half pure white shellac. Apply small amounts of shellac with a brush to the pine needle coils. Do not reuse the mixture. It is important to mix a new solution each time to prevent yellowing of the shellac on the basket.

I have recently discovered shellac comes in a flake form. To use this, mix 2 oz. of shellac flakes to 12 or 16 oz. of denatured alcohol. Mix it in a dark plastic container to prevent it from yellowing. Soak the shellac flakes with the denatured alcohol overnight, or at least eight hours. Don't forget to sign your creation. A tag or a signature object can be attached as your trademark. You may want to start a photo album with all the beautiful pictures you've taken of your baskets. Some basketmakers number and catalog their baskets, while others name them and place in a photo album.

# Pine Needle Basket Patterns

## SMALL BEADED BASKET

*"Precious"*

## Supplies:

| | |
|---|---|
| Size 16 embroidery needle | Pine needles |
| 1 strand (54 beads) 3 mm faceted beads | Raffia |

1. Start with a small pine needle wrapped beginning. Use a smaller coil for this basket for a more delicate look.
2. Using the wheat stitch, coil a flat disk six rows to about 1¾ inches in diameter.
3. Lay Row 7 to start up the sides with a flair. Coil up with a slight flair about seven rows to equal about 1 inch.
4. Change to the swirling pattern of the wheat stitch for the next three rows. Add a 3mm faceted bead on the slant portion of your stitch. Angle the coils toward the middle of the basket.
5. Continue with the wheat stitch for three more rows. Complete the last row with the fern stitch.

# WALNUT TRAY

## Supplies:

| | |
|---|---|
| 3 black walnut slices | Raffia |
| Size 16 embroidery needle | Pine needles |

1. Start your coil on a black walnut slice.
2. Using the wheat stitch, coil a flat disk eleven rows to approximately 4½ inches in diameter.
3. Lay Row 12 to start up the sides at a slant. Work up the sides ten rows to about 1¼ inches high.
4. Lay Row 21 to the outside to create a lip.
5. Wrap a coil of pine needles to create an extension approximately 6½ inches long.
6. Attach walnut slices to each end of the basket. Secure walnut slices with the extensions.
7. On Row 22, use the wheat stitch.
8. On Row 23, finish with the fern stitch.
9. Fill in open spaces with the fagoting stitch.

# BONE BEAD SMALL TRAY

## Supplies:

3, 16mm bone disc beads          Pine needles
Size 16 embroidery needle        Raffia
Seed beads (optional)

1. If desired, add seed beads in the middle of the bone disc beads.
2. Using the swirling wheat stitch, coil a flat disc seven rows, or 2 inches in diameter. Use a smaller coil for this smaller and delicate tray.
3. Lay Row 8 to flair out the sides. Continue using the swirling wheat stitch for seven rows, or approximately 1 inch.
4. Place one bone bead on each side of the basket, directly across form each other. With raffia, attach the bone bead to the previous row stitched.
5. On the next and last row, wrap a pine needle extension on each side, about 6 inches each. The coil will come up to hold the bone bead in place.
6. Secure the coil. Leave a 1-inch space at the midline. Complete the last row.
7. Attach the bone beads to the wrapped extensions. Fill in the open spaces with the fagoting stitch, using the holes in the bone bead.

*Note: The swirling wheat stitch is not a decorative stitch on the outside. This small tray is made so the focus is on the inside of the basket.*

# ANTLER BASKET

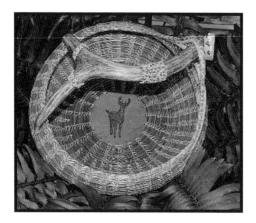

*"Silent Tracks"*

## Supplies:

3-inch leather disc

Permanent ink, brown

Wood burning tool

1/2-inch leather strip

Forked deer antler (mine is 11 inches)

2 strands size 11 seed beads, blue tone

Nymo beading thread

Size 16 embroidery needle

Pine needles

Raffia

Deer Stamp

Dremel tool

Beading needle

3 antler buttons

18 porcupine quills

3/16-inch copper gauge

1. Stamp the deer onto the *center* of the leather disc in permanent brown ink.
2. Outline the edges of the deer stamp with a fine-point wood-burning tool.
3. Place a 1/16-inch drill bit in the Dremel tool. Drill holes around the circumference of the leather disc, 1/2 inch apart, to begin the basket from.
4. Begin your pine needle coil on the leather disc using the wheat stitch and utilizing the pre-drilled holes. You will need to coil your basket according to the size of your antler. The dimensions given are for my 11-inch antler. Measure from the tip of the antler to the end. My base is 6 inches in diameter (this includes the leather disc)
5. Start up the sides with a slight flair to approximately 2½ inches. Taper the coils toward the midline for 2 inches.
6. For the last three rows, use the fern stitch for added strength. *Keep your antler handy—adjust the basket to fit your antler.*
7. Begin the fern stitch. Hold your basket so the deer is facing you. To your right side, wrap your coil with raffia for 2 inches and secure.

8. Continue to wrap an extension to approximately 8½ inches long. Secure about 6½ inches from the last attachment. The open space should be about two inches tall in the middle.

9. Wrap your coil for 2 inches more and secure again. Continue around with the fern stitch. Come back around to the start of the wrapped coil.

10. With a 1/16 inch drill bit in the Dremel tool, drill a hole through the antler tip from side to side (not front to back).

11. Lay the end of the antler on top of the wrapped extension. Adjust the tips of the antler across the basket to make a nice handle. Have the deer stamp facing you when you adjust the antler. With a needle and raffia, attach the tips of the antler, utilizing the predrilled holes.

12. Continue around with the fern stitch. Attach your coils to the previous wrapped extension. Coil up the extension for about 4¾ inches.

13. Wrap another extension approximately 4¾ inches long. Make sure it is long enough to go over the top of your antler.

14. Secure the extension and continue around with the fern stitch. Come up and over with your coil around the last antler extension. Come back around to the beginning of the first wrapped extension and end the basket.

15. Use your imagination to personalize your antler basket. I added seed beads using the peyote stitch around the middle of the antler and at the beginning of each fork. I used a leather strip with porcupine quills in the shape of a V to cover the antler end and then added seed beads at the point of each V.

16. Use the fagoting stitch to fill in the open spaces around the antler. In the large open space, I used three antler buttons decorated with porcupine quills and seed beads.

17. Drill holes 1/4 inch apart around the edge of each antler button. Use these holes to add the buttons with the fagoting stitch. The three buttons are placed in the center. You may also decorate a piece of leather and add it in the open space. Don't forget to sign your masterpiece.

# PINE NEEDLE BRACELET

## Supplies:

1 bracelet form (6¼ inches by 1/4 inch)  Pine needles

Sinew, natural or colored  Shellac, white

Raffia or waxed linen  5, 6 mm beads

Size 6 tapestry needle  Denatured alcohol

Size 13 beading needle  Size 11 seed beads

Disposable paintbrush

1. Double buttonhole wrap the bracelet form using your choice of thread (raffia, waxed linen, or sinew).
2. Find the midline of the bracelet. Attach the sinew utilizing the buttonholes, inside the frame, coming out at the midline.
3. Add a 6 mm bead. With your thread, come out directly across the form. Work to the right and go through one buttonhole with needle and thread.
4. Add a seed bead to the fagoting stitch two times. Go through the next buttonhole and add the next 6mm bead. Repeat with the third 6mm bead.
5. Continue adding the seed beads to the fagoting stitch until you have three on the top and three on the bottom. Finish the open space with the fagoting stitch.
6. Repeat the process to complete the left side.
7. Gently bend the wire form to fit around your wrist. Start your pine needle coil at one end of the frame utilizing the outside buttonhole loops.
8. Use the wheat stitch for the first row.
9. Use the fern stitch for the second and last row.
10. Coat your bracelet to protect it. Mix equal parts of denatured alcohol and white shellac. Paint it on the pine needle coils with a disposable paintbrush.

# FIGURE EIGHT TRAY

## Supplies:

Figure eight wire shape (2¼ inches)  
Size 11 seed beads, clear gold  
Size 13 beading needle  
Size 16 embroidery needle  

2, 1-inch rings  
Raffia  
Pine needles  

1. Buttonhole wrap the figure eight wire shape and the 1-inch rings.
2. Teneriffe weave an arrow pattern in the figure eight. Work an arrow pattern with three arrows in each wire ring.
3. Attach the two rings on each side of the figure eight, utilizing the buttonhole loops.
4. Attach the pine needle coil to the figure eight base. Using the swirling wheat stitch, coil a flat disk for thirteen rows to approximately 5¼ inches.
5. Flair out the sides using the wheat stitch for twelve rows to about 1½ inches.

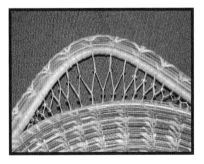

6. Lay Row 26 to the outside to form a lip. Wrap a 4¾-inch pine needle extension on each oblong side. Secure the extensions with a 1-inch space at the midline.
7. Coil two more rows, using the fern stitch on the last row.
8. Fill in the open spaces around the figure eight with the fagoting stitch.
9. Add gold seed beads to the fagoting stitch in the open extensions.

# TURQUOISE TULIP BASKET AND LID

## Supplies:

Size 16 embroidery needle

7x9mm CZ tulip bead, turquoise

6-inch, 34-gauge craft wire

Size 12, three-cut (SC) bead, turquoise

3/4-inch ring

Raffia

Pine Needles

## BASKET

1. With raffia, buttonhole wrap a 3/4-inch ring.
2. Work a teneriffe three-leaf swirl pattern in the center. Use a small coil for this smaller basket.
3. Coil a flat disk for five rows using the wheat stitch, to approximately 2 inches in diameter.
4. Lay Row 6 to come up straight on the sides for six rows, to about 1 inch.
5. At Row 12, change to the swirling wheat stitch.
6. On the slant portion of the stitch, add one three-cut bead. Slightly lay these coils toward the middle of the basket. Add beads for three rows.
7. Switch back to the wheat stitch for four more rows, laying the coils to come straight up the sides.
8. Complete the last row using the fern stitch. The total height of the basket is 2 inches.

## LID

1. Begin with a very small wrapped pine needle coil.
2. Using the swirling wheat stitch, coil out to about 1/4 inch.
3. Add a three-cut bead to the slant portion of the stitch for three rows.
4. Complete the top coiled disk with two more rows to approximately 3/4 inch.
5. Measure the lid disk to match the top opening of the basket base.
6. Lay the coil down to begin the lip. Coil straight down for three rows. On the third row, complete with the fern stitch.
7. Attach the tulip bead with craft wire. With the wire, come up through the beginning hole on the inside of the lid, leaving a tail.
8. Add the tulip bead and one three-cut bead and come back down through the tulip bead again. Come out the beginning hole to the inside of the lid. Tightly twist the wire together with the tail left.
9. Clip away the excess wire and tuck the ends toward the wrapped beginning.

# PINE NEEDLE PENDANT

## Supplies:

Pine needles

Size 13 beading needle

Size 6 tapestry needle

Size B Nymo bead thread,

3-ply waxed linen, plum

4x6mm teardrop bead, amethyst

4mm square beads, kelly green matte

Sot Flex wire, desired length of necklace,
    plus 5 inches

Size 11 seed beads, two contrasting colors
    (opaque, dark purple matte and emerald matte)

Porcupine quills

2 crimp beads

Crimper tool

1 pewter S type clasp

Stiff felt (color to match)

Size 6 Rocaille, amethyst matte

Ultra Suede 2-inch circle
    (color to match)

## PENDANT

1. Soak three clusters of pine needles until very pliable. Rub off most of the nub that joins the pine needle cluster. Leave just enough to keep it together on one cluster only. The other clusters will be separated into three pine needles.

2. With a yard's length of 3-ply waxed linen, thread your tapestry needle, and knot the thread.

3. Coil the nub end of your pine needle cluster in a small circle (approximately 1/4 inch diameter), and bring the needle up through the center of the coil to begin wrapping. It is important to hold onto the coil until you have wrapped it.

4. Catch the threads in the center to fill in the hole as you go through the center. Wrap until the coil is covered and end with your thread under the needles.

5. Continue bending the pine needles around the coil, stitching through the pine needles and the stitch below on the previous row to produce a spiral design. Make eight to ten evenly-spaced stitches on each round.

6. Start adding the second cluster of pine needles one at a time about your second row of stitches. Coil a disc 1½ inches in diameter. (You may not need your third cluster of pine needles.) After the disc is the desired size, taper the coil to an end.

## BEADING AROUND THE PENDANT

1. Cut a 4-inch diameter piece of stiff felt just a little larger than your coiled pendant.

2. Center the coil. Use your beading needle and Nymo thread to tack it to the felt with a few tiny stitches—just enough to hold it in place.

3. Begin beading by placing the first ring of seed beads against the pendant. Thread the beading needle with Nymo thread. Knot the end and bring it up through the felt, next to the coil.

4. String three seed beads of your main color and bring the needle down through the felt right after the last bead. Come back up between the first and second bead and go through the last two beads again.

5. Add three more seed beads and repeat around the coil.

6. Place the second row next to the first, using your contrasting seed bead color.

7. For Row 3, use the main color again.

8. Carefully trim your felt close to the beads. Cut from the back so you won't cut any threads!

9. Cut a piece of ultra suede the size of the beaded pendant coil. Cut a length of Soft Flex 5 inches longer than the desired length of your necklace.

10. As you bead the edge of the pendant, catch the middle of the Soft Flex between the stitches and the edging beads. Have equal lengths of the Soft Flex extending from the disk at 10 o'clock and 2 o'clock.

11. Back the pendant coil with ultra suede using the edging stitch with your main color of seed beads. Bring the needle through the suede and felt from the back to the front and pick up three seed beads. Go down through the last bead strung on, toward the middle one.

12. Pick up two seed beads with each new stitch and stitch around the rest of the circle.

13. End by picking up one seed bead and going down through the first bead stitched. Knot the thread securely and cut off the excess thread.

## NECKLACE

1. String the necklace beads and porcupine quills on the Soft Flex as desired.

2. Finish each end by stringing on a crimp bead, then half of the clasp, and going back through the crimp bead and a few necklace beads.

3. Tighten the Soft Flex and flatten the crimp bead with crimper tool.

4. Cut off the excess Soft Flex.

## DANGLES

1. Make fifteen graduated dangles on the bottom. Start with the longest one in the center of the pendant.

2. Anchor the Nymo thread securely on the back and bring it out the center edge bead. String the dangle beads as desired and bring the needle back through all beads after the square bead (see picture below).

3. Go through the next edge bead to begin the next dangle.

# PORCUPINE QUILL BASKET WITH LID

## Supplies:

2 black walnut slices
3/16-inch copper gauge
Size 6 embroidery needle
Size 11 seed beads, earth tone

Size 13 beading needle
24, 1/4-inch porcupine quills
Raffia and sinew
Pine needle

## BASKET

1. Start your pine needle coil on a black walnut slice.
2. Coil a flat disk using the wheat stitch for sixteen rows, to about 7 inches.
3. Lay Row 17 to start up the sides. Slightly flair up the sides for twelve rows to approximately 2½ inches high.
4. Lay Row 30 toward the middle of the basket. Angle the next five rows toward the midline.
5. Complete the last row with the fern stitch. The basket opening should be about 6¾ inches.

LID

1. Begin the lid on a black walnut slice, using the swirling wheat stitch for five rows to approximately 2½ inches.

2. Lay the coils to come straight down the sides for seven rows to about 1½ inches.

3. Taper the coils in for five rows, then lay the coils to the outside to coil a flat disk.

4. Stop the coil when it is just inside the last row of the basket base. **Do not end your coil.**

5. Start a new coil about pencil size on the inside of your last row on the lid. Coil straight down for three rows and taper the last coil down to end it.

6. Go back to the coil you saved. Continue around until the lid is flush with the base.

7. Wrap a 4½-inch extension coil on opposite sides on the oblong sides. Attach each coil with a 1/2-inch opening at the center.

8. Continue around for one more row, ending with the fern stitch.

9. Fill in the open space using sinew, starting at the midline. Using a beading needle, place one seed bead and a 1/4-inch diameter porcupine quill.

10. Place the quills in a V shape, adding seed beads at each end of the V.

11. Continue to the edge using the fagoting stitch, adding seed beads as you go. Place the bead on your sinew, take your stitch, and come back through the bead.

12. Repeat again from the midline. Fill in the open space on the opposite side in the same manner.

# Section Two

## Gourd Basketry

# GOURDS

The use of gourds, the only known plants to have existed worldwide in prehistoric times, dates back almost as far as woven baskets. They are commonly referred to as nature's pottery and were one of the first cultivated crops. Their relatives are squash, cucumbers, and melons.

Ornamental gourds are often referred to as Mother Nature's showoffs. In autumn, they appear in your local supermarkets or produce stands. They come in a variety of sizes and shapes and are mostly sought after for their dramatic colors. Their shells are generally too thin and fragile for basketmaking.

Instead, hard-shelled gourds are used to make baskets. The durable shell was most significant to early humans. They used these gourds as water dippers, ladles, bowls, storage containers, drums, rattles, and other useful instruments. Gourds have been known to last for thousands of years. The most common hard-shelled gourds used for basketmaking are the Canteen, Corsican Flat, Birdhouse, and Miniature Bottle.

The beginning gardener can grow gourds. They require plenty of sun, well-fertilized soil, and lots of water, especially when the fruit is developing. Gourds need 120 to 140 frost-free days to mature. It is possible to start the plants indoors and then transplant them. Be sure to place them in an area that gets full sun. They are natural climbers and are well suited for trellises.

You must remember not to pick your gourds early, when they have reached the "right" size. They need to remain on the vine until they are fully mature. The stem will turn brown and the tendrils near the ground will go completely dry. A lot of farmers prefer to let gourds dry naturally right in the fields.

If you choose to harvest gourds, store them spread on a wire mesh in an area with good ventilation so the moisture inside them can evaporate. It is advisable to wash them with a weak solution of laundry soap and a little bleach to remove the garden dirt and any possible bacteria or pests. You may want to rotate your gourds in the drying process to prevent soft spots.

Unless a gourd has a soft spot, don't be concerned if mold appears. After the gourd is dry, the mold can be washed off with a mild detergent and a copper kitchen scrubber. A gourd may take from three to six months to dry completely.

## Gathering and Preparing Gourds

Unfortunately, I do not live in an area where the growing season is long enough for hard-shelled gourds. So, I take a little vacation around February and head to Arizona. I enjoy going to the flea markets and craft bazaars looking for gourds. You can rummage through boxes full of gourds and just imagine what a beautiful vessel it will make. There is nothing like eyeing and inspecting a gourd!

Once you have selected your gourd, it will probably need a good bath. Mix up some soapy water and let the gourd soak for about twenty minutes. Gourds float, so you will want to hold it down with a weighted cover. After it has soaked, take a copper scrubber and scrub the shell. If there is a stubborn spot, you may try a little household cleaner. Allow it to stand for several minutes and scrub again. Rinse your gourd and then allow it dry.

With a pencil, draw a line around the gourd where you would like to begin your basket. In the early days, people would use sharpened shells, stones, or bone to cut the gourds. Today we have other choices! An X-Acto hobby tool with a saw blade allows you to cut delicate, fine lines.

*Inhalation of gourd dust is a health hazard. It can lead to sinusitis, emphysema, asthma, and other respiratory problems. So, always remember to wear a mask!*

**After putting on a mask**, begin by rocking the point of the saw blade back and forth to puncture the gourd. You may also use a sharp knife to puncture the beginning hole. Brace the gourd on a foam pad in your lap and carefully cut along your pencil mark.

If you are using the Minicraft Jigsaw, drill a small hole with your Dremel tool. Insert the jigsaw blade in your opening and saw along your pencil mark.

After you have completed your cutting, remove the top of the gourd. Inside you will find dried pulp and seeds. These need to be removed. Use your hands to remove the larger parts and an old spoon to scrape the interior. A small wire brush and rough piece of sandpaper will help smooth the inside surface. Make the inside of the gourd as smooth as possible.

## Exterior Treatment

The choices you have are endless. You may wood burn a design, paint a design with acrylic paints, or simply coat the exterior with Angelus leather dye in your choice of colors. Apply a coat of clear Deft wood spray for a protective coat after wood burning, leather dye, and acrylic paint designs. You may also decide to use Krylon's Make It Stone! paint. It comes with its own clear protective coat. Just make sure the gourd's exterior is clean before you begin any treatment or decoration.

## Interior Treatment

At this time, decide how you will finish the interior. You may leave it as is, or I prefer a more finished look such as Make it Stone! The kit comes in different colors and includes the stone coat and the clear protector coat. Follow the manufacturer's directions to apply. If you decide to use Make It Stone! you should apply it before designing the exterior.

Another choice for a natural finished look is with mulberry paper. Tissue or homemade paper may also be used. Choose a color that will flatter your basket. Earth tone colors help maintain a natural look. Tear the paper into about two-inch pieces. Look for Scenic Cement at your local craft store. This is also used a lot in model train layouts. I use Woodland Scenic, matte formula. With a large stencil brush, dab the Scenic Cement onto the smooth gourd interior, working with a small section at a time. Beginning with a small area, overlap the paper pieces and apply another coat of Scenic Cement over the paper with a slight pounding pressure.

Repeat, working in a small area until the interior is covered. Let the gourd dry overnight. **This method should be done AFTER you have started your basket coils.** By using the mulberry paper, you get a very nice finished touch. The paper will hide the stitches made from starting your coils.

## Materials and Supplies

Listed below are some general supplies you may find helpful. You may not need all of them for each project. If you are testing the waters to see if gourd art is for you, I would recommend the X-Acto hobby tool with a saw blade. If you are already addicted to gourds, I highly recommend the Minicraft jigsaw. It is well worth the investment. **Remember to wear a mask when sawing your gourds.**

Gourds may be purchased at flea markets, produce stands, farmer's markets, some craft stores, and via the Internet. For more information, contact the American Gourd Society.

Your favorite gourd
Deft wood spray
Dremel tool
Wood-burning kit
Dish soap
Krylon spray paint (Make It Stone!)
Old spoon
Wire brush
Dust mask
Pencil (with a good eraser)
X-Acto hobby tool with a saw blade,
    or the Minicraft jigsaw
Sewing needle, size 6 tapestry
    needle, or a size 16 embroidery needle

Angelus or Fieblings leather dye
Glue (G-S Hypo cement)
Deco Art sandstones
Scenic Cement (Woodland Scenic)
Acrylic paints
Copper kitchen scrubber
Beads (for embellishment)
Large stencil brush
Paint brush
Sandpaper
Pine needles
Raffia, waxed linen,
    or artificial sinew
Raffia, waxed linen,
    or artificial sinew

# Gourd Vessel Patterns

## GOURD VESSEL

*"Girlie"*

## Supplies:

1 gourd about 12 inches in diameter

3-ply waxed linen, pink

Make it Stone!, rose quartz

Protective coat spray, clear

G-S Hypo cement glue

1 strand size 6 Rocaille beads, silk pink

1 strand size 11 seed beads, silk red grape

Pine needles

Dremel tool

1 focal bead

1 feather, white

Leather dye, tan

Size 6 tapestry needle

### GOURD

1. Make a pencil mark around the gourd base, approximately 2 inches tall.
2. **Wearing your mask**, cut along the pencil mark. Save the top for another use.
3. Clean the inside of the gourd, making it as smooth as possible.
4. Place the 1/16-inch drill bit in the Dremel tool. Drill holes 1/8 inch from the edge and 1/2 inch apart around the cut edge of the gourd.

INSIDE VIEW

1. Spray inside with the Make it Stone! Let dry and spray with the protective coat.
2. Coat the exterior with the tan leather dye. Let it dry and spray with the protective coat.
3. Lay your pine needle coil along the cut edge of the gourd. Coil up two rows using the chain stitch. Taper the coil to end.

ADDING THE BEADS

1. Start with an arm's length of waxed linen. Double knot the end. Add one seed bead and one size 6 bead and push them down to the knot.
2. Pass the waxed linen from the front to the back in one of the predrilled holes. Pull until the beads rest up against the gourd.
3. Bring the waxed linen out the neighboring hole and add one size 6 bead and one seed bead. Slide the beads up to rest against the gourd and double knot the end. (Place a needle in the center of the knot before you pull it tight and use the needle to help you slide the knot up against the seed bead.)
4. Clip the thread, leaving a 1/8-inch tail. Repeat around the gourd.
5. Dab some G-S Hypo cement on each knot and trim the thread close to the bead, leaving a slight tail.
6. Add the focal bead and decorate with waxed linen. Separate the strands and add seed beads. Twirl the strands around a needle to give them a twisted look.
7. Stick a feather in your focal bead.

# MINIATURE GOURD VESSEL

## Supplies:

1 miniature gourd (about 5¼ inches
    at the base, 2½ inches tall)

Embroidery floss, brown

Pine needles

Size 16 embroidery needle

Size 13 beading needle

Delica beads, silver

Size 11 seed beads, brown

Mulberry paper, brown

G-S Hypo cement glue

Protective coat spray, clear

1 small feather

Leather dye, tan

Raffia

Scenic Cement

Stencil brush

Dremel tool

Wood-burning tool

## GOURD

1. Make a pencil mark around the base 1 inch high. Cut around the gourd on your pencil mark. **Remember to wear your mask.**

2. Make a second pencil mark on the top of the gourd. Measure 3/4 inch down from the stem.

3. Cut around on that pencil mark. Discard the midsection.

4. Clean the inside of the gourd, making it as smooth as possible.

5. Coat the base and lid with the tan leather dye. Allow to dry.

6. Spray the base and lid with the protective coat spray. Allow to dry.

7. Insert the 1/16-inch bit into the Dremel tool. Drill holes around the lid ¼ inch apart. Drill the holes on the base 1/2 inch apart.

8. Place a very fine tip in the wood-burning tool. Wood burn dots in a V pattern between the drilled holes. Point the V down on the base and up on the lid.

9. Using the wheat stitch, begin a fine coil on top of the cut edge of the base. Coil straight up the sides for seven rows or 3/4 inch.

10. Complete the last row with the fern stitch.

11. Begin a fine coil on the lid. Using the wheat stitch, coil with a slight slant down. Stop your coil when it is just inside the last row of the basket base. **Do not end your coil.**

12. Start a new coil just inside the lid on your last row. Coil straight down for five very small coils. Adjust the coils to fit inside the base. Make sure your pine needles are very damp and limber for this fine of work.

13. Come back to the coil you left behind. Continue around until the lid is flush with the basket base. You may desire a slight overhang on the lid.

## ADDING THE BEADS

1. Thread a beading needle with one strand of embroidery floss. Double knot the end.

2. Add one seed bead and one Delica bead. Pass the needle and thread from the outside to the inside of the gourd. Pull the thread until the beads rest against the gourd.

3. Bring the needle and thread through the neighboring hole. Add one Delica bead and one seed bead. Knot the thread and slide the knot up secure to the seed bead. (Place a needle in the center of the knot before you pull it tight. Use the needle to help you slide the knot up against the seed bead.) Clip the thread, leaving a 1/8 inch tail.

4. Repeat around the base and the lid. Dab some G-S Hypo cement on each knot and trim the thread close to the bead, leaving a slight tail.

## ADDING THE PAPER

1. To finish the inside, tear the paper into 1/2-inch to 1-inch pieces. Remember, you are working in a very small area.

2. With a small, stiff brush, apply the Scenic Cement to a small section.

3. Place pieces of the torn paper so they overlap one another.

4. With the brush, apply more Scenic Cement with a slight pounding pressure to the paper.

5. Continue until the entire inside of the lid and base are covered. Allow the paper to dry.

6. Wrap some embroidery floss around the base of the stem. Separate the strands.

7. Add some Delica beads to each strand and attach a feather.

# MINI GOURD VESSEL

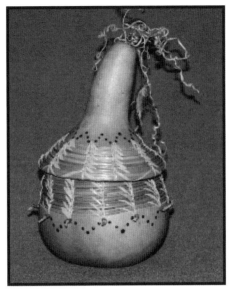

*"Funky"*

## Supplies:

1 miniature gourd (7 inches
   at the base, 4 inches tall)
3-ply waxed linen, blue
Size 16 embroidery needle
Delica beads, red
1 small focal bead
Leather dye, tan
Protective coat spray, clear

G-S Hypo cement glue
Mulberry paper, blue
Scenic Cement
Raffia
Dremel tool
Pine needles
Stencil brush
Wood-burning tool

### GOURD

1. Make a pencil mark around the base 1-inch high. Cut around the gourd on your pencil mark. **Remember to wear your mask.**
2. Make a second pencil mark on the top of the gourd. Measure down from the top of the stem about 1¾ inches. **Wearing your mask,** cut around on the pencil mark. Discard the midsection.
3. Clean the inside of the gourd, making it as smooth as possible.
4. Coat the base and lid with tan leather dye. Allow to dry.
5. Spray the base and lid with protective coat spray. Allow to dry.

6. Insert the 1/16-inch bit into the Dremel tool. Drill holes around the base and lid 1/2 inch apart. Drill a hole through the top of the stem.

7. Place a very fine tip in the wood-burning tool. Wood burn dots in a V pattern between the drilled holes. Point the V down on the base and up on the lid.

8. Begin a fine coil on top of the edge on the base, using the wheat stitch. Coil straight up the side for six rows or 3/4 inch. Complete the last row with the fern stitch.

INSIDE VIEW

1. Begin a small coil on the lid, utilizing the pre-drilled holes. Using the wheat stitch, coil with a slight slant downward. Stop the coil when it is just inside the last row of the basket base. **Do not end your coil.**

2. Start a new coil just inside the lid on your last row. Coil straight down for four very small coils. Adjust the coils to fit inside the base.

3. Come back to the coil you left behind. Continue around until the lid is flush with the basket base. Adjust to fit your taste.

ADDING THE BEADS

1. Start with an arm's length of waxed linen. Double knot one end of the thread.

2. Add one Delica bead. Pass the waxed linen from the front to the inside in one of the predrilled holes. Pull until the bead rests up against the gourd.

3. Bring the waxed linen out the neighboring hole and add one Delica bead. Slide the bead up to rest against the gourd and double knot the end. Clip the thread, leaving a 1/8-inch tail.

4. Repeat around the base. Dab some G-S Hypo cement on each knot and trim the thread close to the beads, leaving slight tails.

## ADDING THE PAPER

1. To finish the inside, tear the paper into 1/2-inch pieces.
2. Working with a small section, use a stiff brush to apply the Scenic Cement to the inside of the gourd.
3. Place the pieces of torn paper over the Scenic Cement so they overlap one another.
4. With the brush, apply more Scenic Cement with a slight pounding pressure to each piece of paper added.
5. Continue until the entire inside of the lid and base are covered. Allow the inside to dry.

## CURLY TOP

1. Cut four strands of waxed linen about 4 inches long and tie the ends together with a knot.
2. Feed all four strands through the pre-drilled hole from the inside of the gourd lid to the outside.
3. Place one small focal bead on the center strand and knot the end of the waxed linen to hold it in place.
4. Separate the strands of waxed linen.
5. Add a Delica bead to each strand at different lengths. Twirl the waxed linen around a needle to give it the funky look.

# BUFFALO GOURD VESSEL

## Supplies:

1 Gourd with stem
    (4 inches tall, 18-inch diameter)
Protective coat spray, clear
3-ply waxed linen, country red or dark rust
Acrylic paints: red, white, and black
Natural paper, neutral color
    (or mulberry paper)
Sandstones by Deco Art, green mist
6mm Rondell beads, garnet
G-S Hypo cement glue
Raffia

Size 16 embroidery needle
Permanent ink, brown
Delica beads, bronze
Pine needles
Buffalo stamp
Scenic Cement
Stencil brush
Dremel tool
Wood-burning tool
Size 6 beads, bronze

## GOURD

1. Make a pencil mark around the gourd base approximately 2 inches tall.
2. Cut the gourd on your pencil mark. **Remember to wear your mask.**
3. Take the top of the gourd and make a second pencil mark around the lid. Measure down about 2½ inches from the stem.
4. **Wearing your mask**, cut again on that pencil mark. Save the middle of the gourd for another use.
5. Clean the inside of the gourd, making it as smooth as possible.

6. Place the 1/16-inch drill bit in the Dremel tool. Drill holes around the base and the lid of the gourd, 1/8 inch from the edge and 1/2 inch apart.

7. Cover the exterior of the lid and the base with sandstone. Follow the manufacturer's directions. For best results, apply two coats. Allow to dry.

8. Using the brown permanent inkpad, stamp the buffalo in the center of the lid. Refer to the picture to paint the design on the buffalo with acrylic paints. (Try the buffalo freehand.) Outline the buffalo using the wood-burning tool.

9. Spray the base and lid with a clear coat of protective spray. Allow to dry.

10. To begin the base, lay your pine needle coil along the cut edge of the bottom of the gourd. Coil straight up the sides, using the wheat stitch.

11. Coil up for five rows. Finish the last row with the fern stitch.

## ADDING THE BEADS

1. Thread a needle with waxed linen and double knot the end.

2. Add one bronze Delica bead, one size 6 bronze bead, and one garnet Rondell bead.

3. Pass the needle and thread from the outside to the inside of the gourd. Pull the thread until the beads rest against the gourd.

4. Bring the needle and thread through the neighboring hole. Add one garnet Rondell bead, one size 6 bronze bead, and one bronze Delica bead.

5. Knot the thread and place the knot up secure to the Delica bead. (Place a needle in the center of the knot before you pull in tight. Use the needle to help you slide the knot up against the Delica bead.) Clip the thread, leaving a 1/8-inch tail.

6. Repeat around the base. Dab some G-S Hypo cement on each knot and trim close to the beads, leaving slight tails.

## LID

1. Lay your pine needle coil along the cut edge of the lid. Using the wheat stitch, coil with a slight slant downward.

2. Stop the coil when it's just inside the last row of the basket base. *Do not end your coil.*

3. Start a new coil about the size of a pencil on the inside of your last row. Coil straight down for about four rows. Adjust the coils so the inside lip fits snugly inside the basket base.

4. Come back to the coil you left behind. Continue around until the lid is flush with the basket base.

5. Complete the last row with the fern stitch.

## ADDING THE PAPER

1.  To finish the inside, tear the paper into approximately 2-inch pieces.
2.  With the stencil brush, apply the Scenic Cement, working with a small section at a time.
3.  Place pieces of the torn paper overlapping one another on top of the Scenic Cement.
4.  With the stencil brush, apply more Scenic Cement on each piece of paper with a slight pounding pressure.
5.  Continue working with a small section until the entire inside of the base and lid are covered. Allow to dry.
6.  Wrap the end of the gourd stem with waxed linen. Separate the strands of the waxed linen.
7.  Add some bronze Delica beads to each strand. Twirl the waxed linen strands around a needle to give them a twisted look.
8.  Apply some buffalo fur at the base of the stem if desired.

# BIBLIOGRAPHY

Armstrong, Katherine L. *Fragrant Basketry: The Pine Needle and Raffia Handbook.* Robson, B.C: Bear Grass Press, 1986.

McFarland, Jeannie. *Pine Needle Raffia Basketry.* Redmond, Oregon: Mid State Printing, Revised 1987.

McFarland, Jeannie. *Advanced Pattern Book For Pine Needle Raffia Basketry.* Redmond, Oregon: Mid State Printing, Revised 1988.

Mallow, Judy Mofield. *Pine Needle Basketry: From Forest Floor to Finished Project.* Asheville, North Carolina: Lark Books, 1996.

Mulford, Judy. *Basic Pine Needle Basketry.* Los Angeles, California: Judy Mulford, 1986.

Summit, Ginger. *Gourds in Your Garden: a guidebook for the home gardener.* Los Altos, California: Hillway Press, 1998.

# ABOUT THE AUTHOR

I have lived in the Pacific Northwest all my life. My husband, Ron, and I reside in Kent, Washington. We share our home with a little cocker spaniel named Betty Cocker and a big ol' tomcat named Fat Chance. Even as a young girl, I enjoyed the outdoors. To me, you have to love the outdoors to be a basketmaker. When walking through the woods, we always come home with something in our pockets to add to a basket! I enjoy gathering just as much as designing and stitching a basket. Hours of time and love are entangled into each piece.

Growing up, we were a "camping family." One particular camping trip inspired me for life. A Native American lady was camped next to us, and I was amazed to see she was making baskets out of pine needles. She noticed I was watching with interest. She took me under her wing and taught me the lost art of Pine Needle Basketry. Little does she know the influence she had on my life. The rest is history...

My baskets have won many awards, including the Grand Champion at the Puyallup Fair. I have shared the art of pine needle and gourd basketry with many of my students. I am also a member of the Northwest Basket Weavers Guild.


Happy Stitching,
Vicky Nickelson